SO-ARN-700

DISCLAIMER. The Empowerment Process® does not claim to produce any specific result. The examples presented are the results reported by individual clients and may not apply to others. For medical advice, contact your health professional.

CREDITS. Cover design: Michael Sutherland and Jeff Poole
Cover photo: Midnight Sun over the Baltic Sea: Fred Swartz
Book photos: Fred and Janet Swartz
Deborah Roberts
Richard Trice

ISBN-13: 978-1499352689
ISBN-10: 1499352689

ACKNOWLEDGEMENTS

I offer heartfelt gratitude to those who have inspired, loved and supported me in my great adventure of life.

To Fred, my wonderfully magical, devoted and ever patient husband and partner in life; to Daniel and Deborah, my beautiful, intelligent, and loving children; to Chloe Faith Wordsworth, my mentor, founder and teacher of Resonance Repatterning; to Maharishi Mahesh Yogi, my spiritual teacher, teacher of the Transcendental Meditation Technique and founder of the Global Country of World Peace; and to all my friends, clients and students who continue to be my teachers daily.

Special thanks to Demerie Faitler who lovingly edited this book, and to Jeff Poole for his marketing expertise.

The Empowerment Process®

*Discover a Powerful Way
to Heal and Transform your Energy*

by Janet Swartz

TABLE OF CONTENTS

Transforming from Within, My Story 2
The Power of Your Beliefs: Anything is Possible 7
Transforming Through the Empowerment Process. 11
Introducing the Principles of the Empowerment Process 15
Investigating and Exploring Your Pathways. 23
Are You Ready to Transform? 27
Applying the Empowerment Process 33
    Moving forward when you have lost your direction 37
    Listening and being heard. 41
    Dealing with overwhelm, fear and anxiety. 45
    Improving your family relationships 49
    Improving your personal and romantic relationships 55
    Managing your weight issues 59
    Opening your creative potential. 63
    Bringing in more financial success 67
    Assisting children through proxy sessions. 71
    How transformations differ from affirmations 75
    Addressing physical health challenges 79
    Finding support to get through your crisis 83
    Staying centered in relationships. 87
    Gaining confidence to recognize and follow your intuition. 91
    Connecting to your spiritual path. 95
Committing to the Journey 99
Your Opportunities with the Empowerment Process. 102
    Individual sessions 102
    Intuitive guidance consultations. 103
    Weekend workshops. 103
    Mentoring programs 104

Transforming from Within, My Story

I am a firm believer in everyone's ability to heal through energetic trans-formation. Although I am not a doctor, nor a medical practitioner of any kind, it is clear to me that personal experience always becomes our opportunity and avenue for learning and healing.

What turned me on to transformational healing came nearly 25 years ago when, at age 40, I was diagnosed with deteriorated cervical discs. My shoulder pain and loss of feeling in my right arm frightened me, and a few days of prednisone was no consolation, only a temporary, mild relief. My prognosis was the sick neck of a 70-year old with a protocol of immediate spinal surgery.

With two young children, being out of commission was not my idea of a good time. Nor was a seemingly risky surgery or the future possibility of becoming stiff-necked with arthritis.

ASK AND YOU SHALL RECEIVE

So, I actually did what my Dad taught me to do as a kid. Pray. I sought an answer from the Heavenly Father, which is how I always see my Maker. "Please send me the information I need to heal myself and be out of pain," were my supplicating thoughts. I was ready to receive an alternative solution.

The result was a phenomenon that I deeply believed in but hardly expected. A communication from the ultimate, invisible Great One gave me several opportunities to explore my healing. I can't say I actually heard God speak, but the next day I learned from a friend about a hands-on healer who was coming to town that week. In addition, another friend gave me the phone number of an herbalist who made his diagnosis long-distance, by phone. The cool thing was that when I made the call he picked up the phone and told me exactly what the MRI showed without any prior information from me.

My belief in intuitive receptivity was immediately switched on. Right away I was blessed to learn that the alternative doctor made a special formula that could heal discs. When I got the nasty tasting powder a few days later, I could immediately feel the knitting going on in my neck, and I knew healing had begun for real. I could handle the nasty taste with the promise of a new neck.

As you might expect from my enthusiasm, the novel hands-on healing experience moved me along even faster. And, just to add more energetics to the mix, I had what's called a Yagya to enliven favorable laws of nature for my healing. This long distance "chanting" by Pundits in India served to move my discomfort out by affecting planetary influences. Wow! Energy healing all the way from across the globe.

Perhaps you'd like to know the results? Within 3 days I was out of pain, off the medication, and after a month or so, I was ready to resume a fairly normal life of picking up my 3 year old and my laundry basket, and carrying in my groceries.

FACING MORE CHALLENGES

Yet, nature had more in store for me. A year and a half later, my 5-year old daughter was diagnosed with cancer, already advanced to stage 4 ½ out of 5. She was carrying a football-size tumor that had eaten her left kidney, and several golf ball size tumors were sitting on her lungs. Although she had to go through 3 major surgeries, 18 months of chemotherapy and radiation treatments, the Whilm's tumor protocol was successful. Western medicine had saved her life. Interestingly enough, the healings I had relied on for myself were not able to cure her.

RECEIVING NEW OPPORTUNITIES

What came during that time was energetic healing work which changed my life and eventually the lives of many others. The first session helped my daughter avoid sickness from the chemo treatments. I was shown how to use "intention" to move beyond my reticence, and convince the Oncologist to reduce the amount of medication to greatly reduce the side effects. In my session, I was able to shift my fears and unconscious belief patterns to resonate with my intention to make the request. Guess what? It worked! It was the first of many sessions which together helped me "survive" the intense heartache of the 2-year protocol and keep my daughter more comfortable as well.

This was just the beginning for me. I took many workshops to learn about positive energy shifts including chakra and meridian balancing, relationship transformation and symbolic work. I became an "expert" in kinesiology and a certified practitioner of Resonance Repatterning.

WORKING WITH MY INTUITION

For fourteen years I was a sought after practitioner, and came to recognize and understand energetic transformation at a very deep level. During this time, my intuition became so refined and accurate that I started to work directly with the energy of others. I no longer had to rely on muscle checking or other references. I would just know intuitively what to say and what they needed for their own empowerment. The surprise for me was that without having had their experience, I could still offer guidance. And, it was clear that it had nothing to do with my left-brain knowledge.

Deep in my heart I knew I had to develop a process to teach others to transform themselves. I loved facilitating positive transformations for my clients, but my deepest desire was to contribute to their self-sufficiency. The summer of 2007, I was challenged to spread the knowledge. Inspired by my current practice as well as The Work of Byron Katie, workshops in the Biology of Belief with Dr. Bruce Lipton, books by Shakti Gawain, Judith Orloff, Penney Peirce, Caroline Myss, Donald Epstein, and others, and with great gratitude to my Transcendental

Meditation teacher, Maharishi Mahesh Yogi, I felt ready to go forward.

THE EMPOWERMENT PROCESS IS BORN

Twenty-four trusting students, including my young adult children and many friends, allowed me to offer my Empowerment Process course which I called *Following Your Intuitive Guidance for Energetic Transformation.* The start was fun, engaging, and packed with knowledge. Shortly afterwards, I took the course on the road as a week-end workshop. The combined energy of all the course participants created a very powerful space for learning and transformation. The two-day, weekend format allowed for time to bring out the necessary knowledge and connect it to the students' own personal experiences. The participants left the course feeling both transformed and empowered to help others.

I feel blessed to be able to travel around the country and teach the process to wonderful, receptive people interested in energetic healing. And I continue to work with individual clients for empowerment process sessions and intuitive readings. My learning is ever expanding.

EMBARKING ON THE JOURNEY

Taking the opportunity to engage with the Empowerment Process continues to open more and more avenues for self-discovery and growth. The possibilities for expanded growth are infinite, the quality of intuitive knowing is always being refined and the tools for transformation are limitless. Embarking on this journey only requires love and compassion for yourself, and a willingness to be open to the transformation process. You will then enjoy a wonderful heart experience for greater fullness and perfect intention in all you do.

The Power of Beliefs:
Anything is Possible

By believing passionately in something that still does not exist, we create it. The nonexistent is whatever we have not sufficiently desired.

Franz Kafka

I would be kidding you if I didn't confess that I believe anything is possible, all healing is possible. What makes me believe this? It partly has to do with my personality. In addition to my many personal experiences of healing, I've witnessed it so many times with my clients and the clients of others. And I have been and continue to be inspired by many books on the subject.

I strongly believe that healing is about communication, communication between our hearts, minds and souls, on the microscopic, macroscopic and divine levels. Yes, the cells, organs, and organ systems are involved; yes, our creative imagination and beliefs are involved; and yes, God and the divine helpers are involved. We, you and I, and all our helpers work together to create energetic healing space for all possibilities.

ALL HEALING COMES FROM WITHIN

There are an infinite number of techniques and practices which have wonderful benefits for improving and sustaining good health. Cures may come from the outside, but all healing comes from within.

One of my favorite books that illustrates the immense possibility of healing and the changes that it brings to our thinking and energy systems is *Dying to Be Me,* by Anita Moorjani. In the book she observes: "I discovered that when my life seems directionless and I feel lost, what it really means is that I've lost my sense of self. I'm not connected with who I truly am and what I've come here to be. This happens when I give my power away to external sources…including cultural and social beliefs."

DRAWING YOUR ANSWERS FROM THE QUESTION

Whenever you have a question, there is a way to draw the answer to you. Otherwise, you wouldn't have had the awareness to even ask the question. Whenever you have pain, the pain is communicating something to you. You can be thankful for the message and begin to look deeply within to understand what is being said.

Western Medicine has many diagnostic tools. However, labeling an illness or disease may do a disfavor if you limit yourself to looking for an outside cure. That is not to say that if there is a life-saving protocol it should be ignored. By all means, go for it. My daughter's life was saved from advanced cancer, a Wilhm's tumor, by following a western protocol, and a heavy-duty one it was. The blessing of life was granted, and beyond that blessing was an opening for energetic healing knowledge that is serving a lifetime purpose for our entire family, and for those with whom we share our knowledge.

TRUSTING YOUR INNER GUIDANCE

How do we know where to start? Where does healing come from? My answer is always this— start from where you are now. Listen to your body, listen to your thoughts and feelings. And listen to your inner guidance, your inner knowing and your intuition. This is what the Empowerment Process accesses for transformation. And, a wonderful by-product of transformational healing is that you get to know yourself and trust the inner guidance that is yours alone.

Transforming Through the Empowerment Process

People cannot be separated from their environment. Living consciousness is not an isolated unit. Human consciousness is increasing the order of the rest of the world and has an incredible power to heal ourselves and the world.

Lynne McTaggart

The Empowerment Process facilitates energetic transformation. It provides non-invasive support for your growth and well-being. Empowerment Process sessions can assist you in your journey by removing the blocks to your full power, opening and unfolding greater insight, creativity, and confidence to help you achieve your highest goals.

TRANSFORMING FOR POSITIVE GROWTH

Whatever aspect of life you feel ready to change presents an opportunity for your growth. Whatever the Universe is wanting for you will arise as new possibilities. Transformation means that you take a step forward from where you are now to a place of greater wholeness, integration, and contentment. In a sense, you are creating a new reality. This growth is experienced as a new energy, a more balanced way of functioning that supports your highest evolution.

The Empowerment Process prepares you to take the next step in your journey. You might be ready to improve your health with a more nutritious diet, timely medical advice, or other support necessary for your healing. You might be ready to change your mental attitude so that your energy is more positive. You might be ready to open to greater spiritual support so that you feel more closely connected to your Divine source. All levels of self-discovery and self-healing lead to self-empowerment through your transformations.

TRANSFORMING FROM THE INSIDE INFLUENCES THE OUTSIDE

As you increase your energetic power, that will be reflected in your thoughts and behavior, and you will uplift the collective energy in your immediate environment and beyond. As you transform from the inside, you will have a very powerful influence on the outside. Feeling more love in your heart creates a warm feeling in your environment, and those around you will respond in kind. That healing energy radiates out into the universe.

If you smile at someone, they will often smile back. When the inner feeling behind your smile is one of genuine happiness, love, and connection, and the other person is willing to take it in, he or she will just pick it up and their whole energy system will respond. Your energy will have created wonderful healing influence. How many times in your life have you said a kind, uplifting word to someone and changed their day? Maybe someone has done that for you.

FULFILLING INTENTIONS

The Empowerment Process is a tool to help you move forward

and make your transformations while you remain centered and grounded. By aligning yourself with what nature has in store for you, accepting your present situation, and being willing to allow change to take place within, you can fulfill your intentions through your transformations. You will become more aware of transformational and healing opportunities for your growth on all levels - physical, mental, emotional and spiritual. The Empowerment Process creates permanent, heightened energy shifts that support your evolution.

Introducing the Principles of the Empowerment Process

You are not a drop in the ocean.
You are the ocean in an entire drop.

Rumi

You and I are living in a world of constant accelerating change. Do you, as an Earth dweller in this time and space take up the challenge to keep up with the movement forward, or choose to hold on to the familiar past? If you close your eyes to global, universal, and personal transformation, are you at risk of getting left behind?

As the world changes at an increasing pace, you'll want to keep up and master your ability to handle and enjoy it. Any resistance to life will restrict your energy, and hold you back. The Empowerment Process gives you the opportunity to address resistances that compromise your mind/body system and expand your own energy.

Through a conscious desire to elicit positive change, you harness the power of your intentions. You will experience a greater wholeness and internal wisdom as you reclaim your power. Judgments, criticisms, and avoidance patterns will be left be-

hind. Transformations will take place according to what you desire if they are in harmony with what the universe wants for you.

ELEMENTS OF TRANSFORMATION WITHIN THE EMPOW-
ERMENT PROCESS

I believe you can turn any obstacle in life into an opportunity for
growth. This belief can become the basis for positive change in
your life. I call the Empowerment Process elements for transformation the 3 A's - Awareness, Acceptance, and Attention.

Awareness

Before you can make any change at all, you need to become
aware of what needs to change. There must be something in
your awareness, some thought or feeling that you want to shift.
You might have some concern, confusion, pain, spiritual issue,
or simply a pivotal point in life. The question simply stated is,
"What's ready for change?"

For example, you might ask, "How can I be more comfortable,
and feel supported and safe in my life?" Without identifying that
there is an issue, there is no possibility of transforming. If there
is no question, there can be no answer.

Many people are unwilling to consider the possibility that there
is an issue because they are afraid that they don't have the
ability to change. If that is your situation, you at least can recognize the fear. That fear may certainly be ready to transform.
The deeper issue is, "I'm afraid I'll never be able to change,"
and the Empowerment Process can transform what holds that
fear in place.

Acceptance

The second aspect is acceptance. If you are challenged with
emotional "overwhelm," physical pain, or feelings of being lost

or in a void, this IS the situation. It is happening. Avoidance of an uncomfortable reality only creates a template for it to resurface at a later date. To sublimate or try to manage with drugs, alcohol, or any addictive behavior only serves to keep the situation at bay for the time being. According to Byron Katie, "loving what is" means to embrace the reality. From there you can transform it.

Sometimes it may be necessary to take medication until the crisis passes. However, once a situation is accepted, then you have the opportunity to be fully present for permanent transformation and healing. It's always a good idea to ask for help when you might need support.

Attention

And, finally, as you put your attention on what you need and want, you will create an intention in the form of an empowering statement. The Empowerment Process will then facilitate an energy shift, enabling you to fulfill your positive intention. Your attention on transforming to a higher, positive and powerful energy supports a permanent change in your physiology. That's the value of the Empowerment Process itself. It sounds simple...and it IS!

THE EMPOWERMENT PROCESS FOLLOWS UNIVERSAL PRINCIPLES.

The Empowerment Process applies universal principles that underlie energetic transformation. These principles inevitably lead to a more consciously awakened and holistic world view. They include:

Principle #1. Your mind, body and spirit are inter-connected.

The Empowerment Process is a holistic process where energy

that shifts on one level allows for shifts to occur on all levels. For example, if you have a safety issue regarding changing careers and you shift this issue, then the confidence to go forward to move into another career option also shifts. This new-found confidence will most likely show up in many other areas of your life such as relationships and decision making.

Recently, a client described to me that she really didn't want to continue teaching in a field that had once been her dream job and a 10-year career. Her teaching contract was being renewed. It gave her financial support and a career focus. But it gave her a headache every time she thought of continuing. She had only two weeks to make her decision whether or not to resign. After an Empowerment Process session, she had the confidence to take a risk and reach out for what she really wanted. The next day she resigned. The day after that, she received an offer in a different field of education that she had been thinking about.

As it turned out, she loves her new position and her teaching team, and the educational goals of the school fully support her skills and talents. She was able to move forward, even though she had no assurance of job security. She has grown to trust her feelings enough to continue to make decisions and even take risks in order to fulfill her desires. As she does, her creative gifts continue to blossom, and she is supported by those around her, an experience that she wasn't having in her former job.

Principle #2. You draw to you what you resonate with.

If you feel, "I am successful," you will draw all kinds of support to you for success. And, the reverse is also true. If you resonate with "I am unable to be successful," you will inhibit your chance of success. The Empowerment Process helps you to identify and shift the limiting beliefs that keep you from being empowered.

One of my clients was unable to meet his financial commitments and was seriously in debt. His goals were unrealistic. He was clearly drawing "lack of success" to his energy field and feeling deflated.

Through the Empowerment Process, he removed the excuses, fears and doubts that were keeping him from seeing realistic goals. He changed his habit of focusing on his worries and fears and moved in a positive direction. Not only did his own creative ideas begin to manifest, but others came to recognize his value and support him. His original distaste for managing his employees changed and it became a pleasure to work with him. Everyone was now on board to fulfill the goals that they mutually agreed on.

Principle #3. You use your power of intention to draw forth what you desire.

Whatever you put your attention on will grow. If you put your attention on worry, fear and doubt, that's what will grow and often manifest. "Worry" is just putting your attention on exactly what you don't want to happen. Dragging around old hurts and beliefs or projecting something you don't want, wastes your enormous potential. You might even feel very tired physically.

Your energy is most powerful when you are fully present. By focusing "here and now" on a situation, you are giving it your full attention, your full energy, and consequently you increase your ability to change for the better. Running from a fear keeps you in a continual state of being chased. Facing a fear and harnessing the power of your own energy allows no room for the chase. The only choice the fear has is to "give up." You can then be free from potential harm. You want to cultivate strength through self-empowerment, rather than project negativity.

Principle #4. Your connection to a greater power is the source of your energy.

Energy shifts that occur through the Empowerment Process can be so amazingly effective that they seem magical. This is because you are able to affect your deepest level of experience at the Quantum energy level. This level is a field of infinite possibilities, where energy has no limits or boundaries and can be used according to your creativity.

In her book, *Peace Pilgrim: Her Life and work In Her Own Words,* the Peace Pilgrim says, "The world may look at you and believe that you are facing great problems, but always there are the inner resources to easily overcome them."

THE EMPOWERMENT PROCESS ALLOWS YOU TO TAP YOUR INNER RESOURCES

Each session creates a step of progress and integration from which to open to the next layer. The Empowerment Process accesses energy and information at all levels - physical, psychological, emotional, and spiritual. What comes to the surface is what your attention is drawn to for transformation. It becomes the focal point for your next step of growth.

As your energy expands and becomes more balanced, you will have the inner support to not only deal with each issue, but to permanently transform the energy behind it. As the feelings, beliefs, unmet needs, and perspectives transform throughout an Empowerment Process, a powerful and obvious integration occurs. You will notice a feeling of peace and completion after the session.

As your energy expands and becomes
more balanced, you will have the inner support
to not only deal with each issue,
but to permanently transform
the energy behind it.

Investigating and Exploring
Your Energy Pathways

Unless we take that first step into the unknown, we will never know our own potential!

Allan Rufus

Only now is Western medical science beginning to understand the relationship between the mind and the body. Stresses and strains in the nervous system can create imbalances in the physiology. The energetic patterns held in the nervous system might have their source in the ancestral DNA, and even in the emotional body carried from lifetime to lifetime. By releasing unwanted and restrictive patterns and beliefs, you can free up more energy, and increase flexibility in the nervous system. This in turn will benefit both your mental outlook and physical health.

Your feelings, beliefs and attitudes are reflected in your thoughts, your body, and your behavior. Feeling overwhelmed or fearful restricts your natural flow of energy and meets resistance. Events will appear threatening and dis-empower you.

A client came to me because he, in his good hearted way, had invited people in to his home who needed a place to stay. Over time they became increasingly demanding and unappreciative. My client didn't want to confront his "guests" for fear of hurting their feelings and causing them stress. However, he was disregarding his own feelings and needs to have his space back. What were the limits of his responsibility? While he enabled his housemates to take over his space, inside he was angry and resentful, even to the point of becoming physically ill.

OPENING ENERGY CHANNELS

After an Empowerment Process session, he was able to communicate without feeling responsible for their intense reactions. He began to feel empowered and relieved at standing his ground and communicating his needs in a kind way. His message was effectively heard.

Un-discharged energy causes damage if it is not released. Now, through the Empowerment Process, you will have the ability to release and transform burdens, heal wounds, and restore balance to your nervous system. Your entire physiology will be supported when you make choices to honestly address and fulfill your needs.

Your entire physiology will be supported
when you make choices to honestly
address and fulfill your needs.

Are You Ready To Transform?

"How does one become a butterfly?" "You must want to fly so much that you are willing to give up being a caterpillar."

Trina Paulus

When life is smooth, you feel a comfortable flow of energy supporting you. But if something happens and the rug is pulled out from under your feet, you may lose your balance and even fall flat on your face. "Get up," you hear a voice inside say, "and begin again." Whether your challenge involves health, finances or relationships, anything that causes stress, you somehow are put to the task of meeting it with a new energetic response.

The Empowerment Process is designed to help you transform your energy to support your positive intentions. You will be able to remove emotional blockages and trapped energy held in the body. Old belief patterns and internal conflicts will no longer hold you back from being fully present in your life.

It may seem like these energetic or emotional responses are holding on to you, but in reality, you have "agreed" to hold on to them. Making the decision to let go of what is disempowering you is the first step to becoming your more powerful, present self.

You might want to take "a leap forward" once you realize there is great, untapped potential inside. Perhaps, external circumstances that in the past demanded your attention will no longer seem so compelling. Committing to growth takes courage, a willingness to be open to change, and the energy to move forward even when you're not sure what lies ahead.

THREE WAYS TO DETERMINE WHEN YOU'RE READY TO TRANSFORM

1. Listen to your "mind-talk."

Recognize repetitive thought patterns that seem to haunt you. You'll be surprised at how much is being revealed by those inner thoughts.

Pay special attention when you find you're:

—comparing yourself with others.

—saying that something or someone will never change.

—feeling impatient for results.

—feeling sorry for yourself

—making excuses for your own or someone else's behavior.

—saying you feel "OK" with something when you actually don't feel good about it at all.

When you keep yourself distracted by daily activities, it is easy to miss the "mind talk" that will give you clues about what you wish to transform. Here are examples of mind talk you might recognize at meal times. "I shouldn't eat this or that," "they shouldn't eat so much," or "I don't have time to eat." Whatever the excuse for being less than present and grateful for your food, there's an opportunity to shift your energy to a higher level of appreciation.

The Empowerment Process helps you become more heart centered and clear about what is happening in the present so that you can move out of your excuses and old habits of thought and behavior. As the caterpillar in the above quote is questioning his new possibilities in anticipation of change, so you can listen to your voice within and be ready to transform.

2. Recognize an emotional imbalance.

How many times have you felt defeated? Life just seems too much to deal with. Perhaps your reaction to an incident has caused you to feel an overpowering negative emotion which continues to weigh on your mind. The longer you hold on to it, the longer it dis-empowers you. That is often the case when family members and friends hold grudges and decide not to communicate. They live with an underlying tension that may well interfere with their life even on a subtle level. If they only knew that misunderstandings and emotional wounds can be resolved by the desire to do so. Love is such a healer.

I find in my own life, if I just patiently stick with what is in front of me without dwelling on what may or may not happen, life has a way of working itself out. A client's cancellation provides the time I need to finish a project; a snow day cancels my exercise class and I am available to receive an important phone call; I'm invited for lunch and don't need to cook that day…the list can go on and on.

If you find that you can't relax and let go of feeling "too much," then the Empowerment Process can help you balance your energy so you become centered and effective again. The Process can assist in removing the underlying belief, "I never get the relaxation time I need." You will have unveiled a more powerful level of energy for inner well-being.

Here's the advice given by Peace Pilgrim in her book, *Her Life and Work in Her Own Words.* "If your life is in harmony with the laws which govern this universe, then life is full and good, and is never overcrowded. If you do feel overwhelmed, you are doing more than is right for you, more than your job in the total scheme of things."

Can you say, "no," if that is in your highest and best interest for health and happiness? Can you say "yes" to change? If so, you are ready to transform.

3. Pay attention to your body's messages.

Your body sends you messages all the time. If you don't listen, the alerts will get stronger until you feel them. They may even begin to compromise your health. Putting your attention on a feeling of discomfort or a specific physical problem is paramount for transformation. You'll usually find an underlying emotional or spiritual issue. If you are compromised physically for a short time or, even a long time, see what opportunity is being offered for your transformation.

Some people have severe disabilities, but because they pay careful attention to the underlying emotional messages and their mental attitudes, their disabilities do not get in their way. My friend, born with only one arm, raised 3 children, and pursued a career as a massage and physical therapist. I am always inspired by people who are not held back by their challenges in life

Other people, who seem to have no reason to complain, are filled with emotional turmoil and self-esteem issues. Their emotions are on the verge of breaking loose and turning into an ulcer, chronic headache or digestive disorder. By addressing the underlying emotions and attitudes, the physical condition may resolve quickly. I have seen this occur many times with my clients. Blood pressure has miraculously normalized, and scars spontaneously healed from a single Empowerment Process session.

Committing to growth takes courage,
a willingness to be open to change,
and the energy to move forward
even when you're not sure what lies ahead.

Applying the Empowerment Process

When you do things from your soul, you feel a river
moving in you, a joy. Rumi

Most transformation starts with a feeling, a discomfort, a concern, or a question.

If you have a question, and you ask it, even if only to yourself, you have activated a process for receiving an answer. I call it the "Infinite Google." As Steve Jobs has said, "If you define the problem correctly, you almost have the solution." Find the comfort and healing you need now.

HOW THE EMPOWERMENT PROCESS CAN HELP YOU

The Empowerment Process is a self-empowerment tool. Although the word empowerment implies a "doing," the actual experience is more like an "undoing." That is, you are relieving your energy system of burdens, worries, and unnecessary constrictions that aren't serving you. The result of your positive transformation through the Empowerment Process is that you feel comfortable living in your own energy space. You start with what is bothering you and move through the feelings, thoughts and attitudes to come to a new perspective. The empowerment is felt throughout your entire being as you integrate the new energy.

In the following chapters, I'll address frequently asked questions from clients and relate some personal examples of their transformations. You may relate to one or more and see for yourself what you might be ready and willing to transform.

If you have a question,
and you ask it,
even if only to yourself,
you have activated a process for
receiving an answer.

Moving Forward When You Have Lost Your Direction

I can't change the direction of the wind, but I can adjust my sails to always reach my destination.

Jimmy Dean

Sometimes you may feel out of sorts, just uncomfortable with life in general. You don't really know what or why something is bothering you. You may intuitively know that big changes are about to happen, but in the meantime you are stuck in an emotional or spiritual, turmoil that feels like a void with no direction.

When you find an opening through the Empowerment Process, you can come to a place of peace. You will understand your experiences and begin to see a new direction. As the clouds move, the sun can peak through and shed its light.

CONTINUING EFFECTS FROM THE PAST

A troublesome issue often surfaces as an emotional discomfort. You no doubt carry a disempowering pattern from a past reaction to a single incident or a series of incidents. Moreover, you have turned your belief about what happened into a story to legitimize it. Unless you have let it go at some earlier point in your life, that story continues to influence you now.

For example, one of my clients felt that her boss didn't appreciate the work she did for her. The credit for her ideas always seemed to go to her co-worker. She kept wondering whether or not she should look for a new job.

When she came to me for an Empowerment Process session, she noticed a general theme in her life of not being appreciated. She felt that even her husband, her kids, and her friends didn't offer appreciation. She remembered that when she was young, no matter what she did to please her Mom, she was never acknowledged or appreciated for it. The specific issue with her boss was indicative of a broader, older scenario from childhood. It provided a mirror for what was ready for transformation. As she was able to acknowledge and accept this pattern, she opened to transforming it through the Empowerment Process.

CREATING A NEW PRESENT REALITY

It became clear during the session that she was valued all along, but her doubts, and beliefs that she didn't deserve being validated blocked her ability to receive positive feedback. In her transformation, she established a higher energy frequency and recognized that she could appreciate herself. That energy was felt by others and they spontaneously began to express their appreciation for her. She in turn began to pay attention to her newfound confidence and notice the positive response of others. They actually received the benefit of her self-assurance. What she had shut out before developed into a new openheartedness, and her quality of life at work, at home, and in all environments brought her a freedom and happiness that she never expected.

It may not be reasonable to expect acknowledgment and appreciation all the time, but if you can feel it within, and project it to others, this heart energy will always be very nourishing and healing. According to a study by Dana Tomasino, researcher at the Institute of Heart Math, the heart's magnetic field is 5000 times stronger than that of the brain, and provides a global synchronization signal for the entire body affecting all the organs and other internal structures. This fact alone gives everyone a reason to cultivate a strong and healthy heart-centered way of functioning. Carlos Castaneda writes, "Does your path have a heart? If it does, the path is good; if it doesn't, it's of no use."

Listening and Being Heard

With the gift of listening comes the gift of healing.

Catherine de Hueck

Everyone wants to be heard. Sharing, expressing emotions and connecting to others, especially those you love, are natural human activities. The Empowerment Process can help you gain clarity and transform issues that prevent you from energetically radiating your message and hearing the other person's message.

COMMUNICATING FROM THE HEART: SHARING AND LISTENING

Communicating from the heart entails both a sharing and listening. You always want to know if and how you are being received. The question is, are you communicating in a way that allows you to be heard by your listener? As a famous Chinese proverb reveals, "The real art of conversation is not only to say the right thing at the right time, but also to leave unsaid the wrong thing at the tempting moment."

The Empowerment Process helps you discover and transform

those things that prevent your message from being received. It may be your own insensitivity to the person you are talking with. Is your expression too harsh and demanding? Are you communicating unreasonable expectations of what you want and prevent the listener from responding honestly? Or maybe, you are carrying an unconscious belief that no one ever listens to you.

Often, an emotional block to being heard stems from not having been listened to at some earlier point in life. Disempowering energy patterns are generally developed during childhood when parents are absorbed in their own problems and disregard or even prevent their child's communication to them. If this was a situation you faced, you might have created a belief that you don't need to be heard in order to be loved, feel safe, or have your needs met. The result might be that you stopped expressing your needs to avoid the disappointment of not getting them met.

What about the person who is unable to listen? When you imagine that the other person is not listening to you, it may be true. What is the cause? When someone's needs are unmet and they are gripped by uncomfortable emotions, it's nearly impossible for them to have the focus to allow outside information in.

RESOLVING PAST ISSUES OF NEVER BEING HEARD

One of my clients came to me saying that her daughter would never listen to her and would literally leave the room whenever she walked in. This avoidance pattern went on for several months causing frustration for both of them. During the Empowerment Process, the mom realized that she was always asking her daughter to do something for her, or she would be checking up on her daughter's homework status, or suggesting that she get ready for bed. The sensitive girl found this behavior to be intrusive and harsh. To protect herself, she just tuned her mother out.

During the transformation process, my client discovered that this emotional avoidance pattern was a generational replay of her own mother's inability to listen to her. Her mother was always looking to get her own needs met, and so my client's feelings were ignored. The message my client was passing on to her own daughter was that she, too, will never feel heard. The Empowerment Process served to break this generational pattern and the mother-daughter relationship was not only repaired, but continues to develop into an open, welcome and active mutual exchange.

The Empowerment Process can help you transform your past unmet needs and beliefs so that you can truly listen — to yourself and to others. At the same time it also opens up channels so that others listen to you as well. The result of your transformation will allow you to listen attentively to others without judgmental and reactive emotional imbalances. As you become more sensitive to others, your communication will be more authentic and rewarding. You will be gratified to know that other people will hear you, and be there for you as you are for them.

Dealing with Overwhelm, Fear and Anxiety

I don't think any amount of fear is healthy... I don't think apprehension can do anything but attract.

Peace Pilgrim

We live in a demanding world, one that often puts us in a position of having to expend more energy than we are able to replace through rest and recreation. Although giving is the basis of receiving, you might feel overwhelmed and anxious about "making it all happen." Earning money, feeding the kids, being on board for friends and other family members who might really need you, can be taxing and energy depleting. In addition, something unexpected may trigger major emotional responses.

You can transform negative emotions and neutralize that gripping feeling of impending "disaster" by attending to the anxiety and worry that often accompany our contemporary life-styles. The Empowerment Process gives you the opportunity to reduce those moments of overwhelm and stabilize yourself for long-term, balanced growth. Extreme tension in the present is an echo of something stored in your physiology from the past, and responses from past traumatic events come up when least expected.

HEALING EMOTIONS FROM THEIR ROOT CAUSE

When you are feeling emotionally overwhelmed or out of control, there is great temptation to take a pill or some anti-anxiety medication. You might feel better and sometimes that is necessary to control extreme feelings and behavior. However, in the long run, it is best to heal your problems at the source. The Empowerment Process is specifically designed to heal the root cause of your problems.

Here is one of my favorite examples of a client turnaround. A 92-year old lady called me in a panic. Her doctor had just told her that her routine blood test indicated a strong "possibility" of cancer. After hearing this news she wasn't able to sleep or calm down for a second, and she had three days to go before hearing the final test results. I quieted her down enough to ask, "Maggie, do you want to suffer if your test comes out fine and you don't have cancer?" "Of course not," she says. "Maggie, do you want to suffer if your test indicates you do have cancer?" Becoming more reflective, she admitted that she didn't want to suffer in either case. So, I knew then she was open for transformation. She was able to move out of the fear and stay in the present. Fortunately, the results were fine, and she felt happy because she didn't "die" from worry.

ACCEPTING YOUR FEELINGS TO RELEASE THE UN-WANTED ENERGY

A key to transforming your fear and anxiety is to fully accept the feeling without trying to avoid it. Painful as that may be, a willingness to face your fear allows you to unblock your energy and move it through your system. The Empowerment Process allows you to identify and release the tension and fear.

You can address and ease the traumas from past events… such as being stuck in a birth canal, hearing negative or inappropriate comments from your mother or father, losing someone close to you, or even something from a past life or ancestral time. Once you are able to release this tension from its source, you will find that you no longer will have to face such emotional intensity even if there is still some residual healing to be done.

The Empowerment Process helps subtle, long-standing anxieties that keep you feeling constricted due to lack of confidence, emotional instability, inability to receive love, or feeling unsafe. Sometimes, a current issue may be very small, but you blow it out of proportion as your unmet needs and old reactive patterns surface. Or, perhaps when you do face circumstances of great importance you are unable to muster your courage for a good response. In either case, your investment in healing becomes paramount to your well-being during these times.

Once you address the source of these concerns, your entire energy system and your way of functioning will dramatically improve. Life will be much easier.

Improving Your Family Relationships

Never let problems to be solved become more important than a person to be loved.

Barbara Johnson

Your family is your most precious and intimate teacher. The Empowerment Process has been helpful in so many ways. It gives parents the opportunity to listen without responding emotionally and allows children to feel safe to open up to their parents. It has given children a new appreciation of their parents without feeling impatient or frustrated by their belief systems. And, it opens the door for spouses, siblings, and all family members to hear one another...living life with an open heart and mind, without forming judgments, needing to be right, or feeling unappreciated. To put it simply—hard hearts are softened.

LISTENING WITHOUT FEAR AND JUDGEMENT

It might seem simple, but for many of us, one of the most difficult challenges is to really hear the other person and take in what they have to say. What you hear might cause some emotional reaction, but that is what you need to take in and resolve internally. You'll want to balance your emotions so you can integrate the message and really hear what is being expressed without judgment or fear. You will feel safe to communicate your true feelings. When you have mastered these two principles, being open to listening and receiving, and being able to express yourself freely without fear, then you can experience a more vibrant and healthy relationship.

I have worked with many couples, both individually and together, who have learned these principles, made the necessary transformations and now have healthy, growing marriages.

GETTING YOUR NEEDS MET

Recently I was facilitating an Empowerment Process session with a very warm fellow who desperately needed to share his love and affection with his wife of many years. However, he expressed feeling "put off" whenever he was asked to do what he felt were trivial chores around the house. He felt afraid to address the situation or mention to her how he felt when she asked him to help. He had no idea how to express his unmet needs to her. And, since she wasn't responding to his love, he was reaching the point where he was thinking of leaving the household.

The Empowerment Process helped him open up blocks from the past that kept him from being sensitive to her, and he became more aware of his own needs as well. He began to perceive that he was living a replay of his younger days when his mother demanded that he do similar chores causing him to feel that he was not unconditionally loved. He was so frustrated at that time that he left home before finishing high school.

Through the Empowerment Process, he was able to release the pent-up frustrated energy and feel unconditionally loved while being ready and willing to help around the house. He could be his authentic self, offer his unconditional love, meet the needs of the family, and draw to himself what he needed. His wife, now feeling supported, was willing to receive his love and share hers more readily with him. Had the healing not taken place, he may have left his home and family as he did as a younger fellow, only to repeat the same pattern again, with someone else.

The opportunity for growth often surfaces with the people you love the most.

Why throw away this opportunity?

If you have an anger issue, tend to be impatient, or are unable to have a heart connection with a family member, then it's best to address and transform your own issues. You'll be surprised how a change in your energy also changes others. As you start to respond positively to others they will do so in turn and the tone of your family life will become more harmonious.

OPENING TO UNCONDITIONAL LOVE

If your son, for example, continually comes home intoxicated, rather than yell at him and take away his privileges, try looking beyond his behavior and listening to his feelings. If you tend to speak or act inappropriately because your emotional hot buttons are pushed, the Empowerment Process can help you remove these trigger points. Then you can more easily engage in a discussion to find out how he is, what he needs, and how you can help. Imagine the relief he might feel if you are on his team.

After the fact, apologies and forgiveness are fine, but if the core behavior doesn't change, over time the family relationships wear down and deteriorate, and the issues still remain. It's best to protect your children or any family member from hurt caused by any inadvertent abuse or manipulative behavior from you. As Maharishi Mahesh Yogi so beautifully encapsulates the message in a talk: "Love knows that nothing is ever needed but more love. It is what we all do with our hearts that affects others most deeply. It is not the movements of our body or the words within our mind that transmits love. We love from heart to heart."

Through the Empowerment Process, as you change your energy field, you will naturally become more nurturing. Once pent up anger, fear and frustration are released and the underlying beliefs are transformed, forgiveness, unconditional love and more nurturing behavior becomes automatic.

Your family is your most precious
and intimate teacher.
Live life with an open heart and mind.
without judgment, fear, or needing to be right.

Improving your Personal and Romantic Relationships

If you love somebody, let them go; for if they return, they were always yours. And if they don't, they never were.

Kahlil Gibran

People of all ages, from teens to seniors, come to me with concerns about their personal and romantic relationships. Issues often arise when they feel misunderstood or mistreated. In most cases they are confused about their feelings and unsure about how to communicate in their intimate relationships.

FEELING SAFE IN RELATIONSHIP

In every relationship there is a need to share feelings, ideas, and reactions with the other person. When expressing a concern, you need to feel safe, especially if the other person tends to be either emotionally delicate or explosive. Sometimes it is not easy to take the important step of standing up for yourself while maintaining a gentle and honest demeanor. However, by establishing clear communication and behavioral boundaries in your relationship, you will create the appropriate atmosphere to share your feelings.

At times within your relationship, you will need to support the other person's emotional issues. It's fine to accept that role as long as you don't compromise your own well-being. That is, you're careful that they don't use you to just unload emotional baggage. The Empowerment Process can help you transform any fears or concerns about expressing yourself in a clear, loving way as well as make decisions about your responsibility to support the other person.

ADDRESSING YOUR REACTIONS

It is important to remember that you can't change another person, you can only change yourself. If you find yourself in a tough situation where you feel you aren't being treated properly, you'll need to address your own reactions to the situation.

Even when in love with someone, you may be a victim of abuse. In such a relationship, it's important to ask yourself what qualities you resonate with and display that somehow allow you to be a victim. There is certainly a boundary issue. Are you unable to stand up for yourself? Do you let others take advantage of you? If so, you may very well be holding onto unconscious beliefs that draw physical or emotional abuse to you.

The Empowerment Process is designed to help shift long-held disempowering beliefs that underlie your situation such as "I am unworthy of being unconditionally loved," "I am unappreciated," or "I can't get what I need." Challenges that come to you in life can offer big opportunities for positive change, change that may be necessary to ensure harmony and even safety in daily life.

HAVING THE STRENGTH TO BE IN AN APPROPRIATE RELATIONSHIP

Sometimes people are faced with the decision whether or not

to leave a relationship. The situation is complicated when they still feel love for the person. The sense of impending loss, grief, guilt, or loneliness may be overwhelming. Discovering inner strength and self-love is necessary to go forward.

One of my clients was confused and feeling the need to choose between two men in her life. The way she saw it, she either had to continue with a fellow who wouldn't make a permanent commitment to her but who was fun and playful, or commit to a stable fellow who wanted to marry her but didn't offer the same adventuresome spirit she was so attracted to.

When I asked her how she felt about a third choice, being alone, she wasn't willing to consider it. In fact that possibility caused her to feel fear and panic. She claimed that none of her needs would be met without a loving partnership.

STAYING TRUE TO YOUR VALUES

The Empowerment Process was a blessing at this point. It helped her as she moved through the panic and fear and a need for immediate security. She was able to recognize and reconnect with her deepest desires for inner stability and spiritual evolution, and stay true to her progressive life values. After years of turmoil, she could finally break free of old habits that kept her re-living old painful behavior patterns. She realized that neither man was right for her and that she did not need to compromise her values in exchange for security.

Removing the blocks that keep you in a compromised state gives you a wonderful opportunity to live a more powerful level of inner well-being. As you clear yourself of emotional baggage and unmet needs, the ability to communicate and make decisions about relationships improves. When expectations and needs are resolved at a fundamental level, heartfelt expression of genuine love and appreciation comes naturally.

Managing Your Weight

We have far more control over our health and the condition of
our bodies than we ever thought possible.

Mike Rabe

It's a great challenge for many of us to keep our weight at a comfortable, aesthetically pleasing level. Some people are very bothered by gaining a pound or two, while others seem to feel OK even 20 or 30 pounds higher than what doctors recommend. The key here is about a healthy weight as well as a healthy attitude about maintaining it.

ADDRESSING EMOTIONAL ISSUES

Experts estimate that 75% of the time overeating is caused by emotions. The Empowerment Process can help you manage and control weight issues by transforming your emotionally based eating habits and beliefs about yourself. The expressions, "you are what you eat," and, "you are what you think," are intimately connected.

Depression, boredom, loneliness, chronic anger, anxiety, frustration, stress, relationship problems and poor self-esteem can result in overeating and unwanted weight gain. And for some, it's the opposite. Eating becomes a source of anxiety and the result is too much weight loss. These are the emotional issues that you can address and transform through the Empowerment Process.

Emotional eating becomes an avoidance habit, preventing you from learning skills that could effectively resolve your emotional distress. The Empowerment Process helps identify the disempowering thoughts that trigger your emotional eating. Then food and weight gain are no longer issues. Once you have identified what triggers your need for comfort through food, you are in a position to break that habit.

MEETING YOUR NEEDS FOR A HEALTHY LIFESTYLE

During an Empowerment Process, one of my clients identified the issue "never getting enough." He found that the feeling came from memories of never getting enough love during childhood. He lacked self-esteem. The more he tried to prove his self-worth, the more he ate. The more he ate the less he felt loved. Meeting his needs became a great challenge.

As he transformed this pattern, he opened to receiving love from himself and others. He surrendered to the fact that he didn't need to control his emotions, but rather accept them, and transform them to a healthier state. He then found it easier to address the challenge of losing weight.

It must also be mentioned that other causes of unnecessary weight gain or loss may include the effects of medication or a lack of vital nutrients. You may want to consult your medical advisor about these possibilities. Empower yourself, and go forward with a healthy life-style.

Transforming emotionally based eating habits
allows you to manage your weight
as you effectively resolve
your disempowering beliefs.

Opening Your Creative Potential

You can't use up creativity.
The more you use, the more you have.

Maya Angelou

The Empowerment Process helps you trust your innate creative ability as you let go of doubts and fears.

Because most people are creatures of habit, it's easy to become stuck in old ways of thinking that limit creative possibilities. You become accustomed to linear thinking as the basis for setting goals and solving problems. These limitations constrict your energy flow; exercising creativity becomes a struggle. Letting go of old paradigms allows the creative impulse within you to emerge. Buckminster Fuller, renowned 20th century inventor and visionary, notes, "In order to change an existing paradigm you do not struggle to try and change the problematic model, you create a new model and make the old one obsolete."

LETTING GO OF THE OLD TO LET IN THE NEW

An energetic frequency for letting go of old thinking opens you to receive an organic flow of new ideas. Strike up that frequency and then watch ideas emerge. For example, you have to make a decision and see only two possibilities. Release your old thinking patterns and lo and behold— a third, fourth, or even fifth possibility appears.

Because Empowerment Process transformations take place within your energetic core, you will be able to tap into a place of stillness where infinite possibilities reside. Then creative solutions to problems will spontaneously emerge and offer you a more holistic way to function. A new level of knowledge becomes available.

One of my clients had developed an educational tool to address an auto immune disorder. However, she couldn't seem to get a niche in the market to draw clients to her. Feeling discouraged and financially strapped, she came to me and we worked on her self-esteem and anxiety issues.

FINDING YOUR CREATIVE OUTLET

As she transformed her deep concerns of being overworked and unappreciated, she was able to begin taking risks and move forward. She learned to say "no" to her boss, set realistic boundaries, and open to her own creativity. Soon she secured a position as a trainer in a related business. She now had confidence to put in the time and effort to succeed in this new position, and simultaneously draw interest and support for her own work. She is now moving towards establishing her own business while remaining financially secure and stable in her current job. The challenges she overcame served as a great learning tool to enhance her creative ability to find solutions and encourage her to move forward.

You'll find that through the Empowerment Process you will be able to develop creativity from within your core, "the energetic field of all possibilities." When your perspective shifts, and you transform old beliefs and feelings, the original issue will no longer carry an emotional charge. Enlivening your creativity will give you more energy to fulfill your passion. The flow is infinite. Problems seem small when you have the creative power to solve them.

Bringing in Financial Success

A big part of financial freedom is having your heart and mind free from worry about the what-ifs of life.

Suze Orman

Financial security is a great blessing in life and I am often asked to help people with their concerns about it. Although the focus of The Empowerment Process is often on money, there are usually deeper issues that prevent the inward flow of wealth. Security, a big issue for many people, can give rise to a general sense of "lacking something" which includes financial support.

TRANSFORMING UNDERLYING ISSUES

The habit of worrying, for example, is an energy depleting activity, and may well be triggered by financial issues. Do you have enough money to live comfortably without worrying about paying your bills and taking care of health concerns? As you investigate the issue of how much money is enough for your lifestyle, you may find that somewhere in your belief system you'll either "never have enough," "you are unworthy," or "you'll never be able to support yourself." These examples of limiting beliefs are common and can easily be addressed and transformed through the Empowerment Process.

Recently, a client expressed that she was unable to focus on her entrepreneurial goals. Information surfaced during the session that she came from a very large family and had alcoholic parents. Because she was the first to go to college and become financially successful, her family tended to depend on her. Although many years had passed, she continued to feel the need to support everyone. She resonated energetically with the role of being the main support person in the family.

She admitted that she was often tired and under pressure from her huge burden. The conflict between her fulfilling her own needs and fulfilling the needs of everyone else was eating her up inside. Through an Empowerment Process, she started to "believe in herself" and confidently work on her business goals. She stayed focused in the present and made sure she was rested and able to say "no" when appropriate. Once her behavior had changed, she was respected for her decisions, and her family and work associates benefited from her new, more centered way of running her life.

TRANSFORMING FEAR TO MEET SUCCESS

Another common deterrent from meeting financial goals is the fear of success.

Do you intentionally sabotage yourself and mistakenly see good opportunities as dangerous risks? Do you hold back from asking for the help you need to get started? Do you present ideas that are too vague to attract backers for fear that they might actually support you? Do you wear yourself out so that you are too tired to change your situation? The list goes on and on. Ask yourself, are you using your energy to increase your success, or are you wasting it for fear of success? Where is your energy being spent?

Sometimes you can be so openhearted, you give away your time, talents and energy. Perhaps you feel that because you are just starting out you need to share your services for little or no compensation. If you want to establish your credibility and worth, however, you'll need to match your creativity and energy with a practical business plan, and address the issues that hold you back.

Many talented and educated people have a difficult time charging for their services. They give out their knowledge, time, and expertise for little or no money. Often, because it's something they just enjoy doing, they don't think about its monetary value. If they are planning a life of volunteering, and they can afford not to charge, that may be appropriate. However, if that's not the case, finding the market for their services or products and charging their clientele or customers is necessary.

Through the Empowerment Process, you can identify and transform tendencies, on any level, that obstruct your business and financial success. Beliefs about being unworthy, fears of being seen or exposed, and even feeling reluctant to receive any appreciation at all may need to be addressed and transformed. Your worth will continue to increase as you recognize and appreciate your own value. The results will be life-changing and you will be rewarded for sharing your gifts.

Assisting Children with Proxy Sessions

Your children are not your children.
They are the sons and daughters of Life's longing for itself.
They came through you but not from you and though they are
with you yet they belong not to you.

Khalil Gibran

Your children are your teachers. You create life and then you watch them follow their own path of evolution. You have the honor of mentoring and being a compassionate and loving supporter. Maybe you see it as an enormous responsibility as well. Whenever you are emotionally challenged, you may lose your temper and respond inappropriately to them. There are two ways the Empowerment Process can help your children make positive transformations for their well-being.

BEING A PROXY FOR YOUR CHILD'S TRANSFORMATION

The first way I can be helpful is to have you serve as a proxy or energetic substitute for them in order to address their situation or issue. It's as if I'd be working directly with your son or daughter through your energy as you tune into their field. The wonderful thing about energy is that it is not bound by space or time and can even be directed over great distances. You will express your child's concerns as you interpret them, and through you I will facilitate the transformations for their empowerment.

My client's three year old son was afraid of the dark and had a very hard time going to bed. I worked with his Mom as his proxy on his issue. We uncovered a time when he had heard a scary sound and was afraid to get out of bed to wake her for comfort. He imagined harmful boogie men under his bed and didn't want anything to do with being near them. So, he insisted on being in his Mom's bed.

The important thing at this point is to accept and acknowledge his emotion, for then you can help transform it. Saying things like, "just be brave," or "it's just your imagination," only leaves his fear in place and dishonors his emotional reality and even make him reluctant to turn to you for help.

Through the Empowerment Process, we were able to dispel the fear and send the beings away. Her little boy then was assured and confident that he was safe. He bravely tried out his bed again, and peacefully fell asleep. And, Mom could then get some sleep, too.

Unless a child is too young, or unable to respond, it's best to get their verbal permission to go through the Empowerment Process. If this is not possible, as a loving parent with a pure intention, you can proxy for them without their knowledge. This way I am able to assist unborn babies in their birthing process, children going through a surgery, and non-verbal autistic children. Proxy sessions are common in my work as I meet the majority of my clients on the telephone. The results are just as effective as in-person sessions.

TRANSFORMING YOUR CONCERNS ABOUT YOUR CHILD

A second way the Empowerment Process can benefit your children is to work directly with you as their parent. For example, if you are worried about their health, their behavior, or any situation for that matter, I can help you dispel your worry which is of no benefit to either you or them. I can also boost your energy to support them through their challenges.

When my 5-year old went through a two year protocol for cancer, I had energetic transformation sessions so that I could keep myself grounded, emotionally present, and mentally clear during the many medical procedures and caretaking. She, of course, benefited immensely from my ability to be there for her. She also received proxy, healing energy with the intention of helping to bring her fevers down after surgery and bring her blood counts up after chemotherapy, and be open to helping her heal with whatever came next in her treatments.

If you are a parent, you know how important it is to be a good role model. You don't even have to say much, or even anything, if your behavior is appropriate for each situation. The Empowerment Process addresses concerns you might have about being a good example for your child. I really worked diligently to transform my fears of the surgery outcomes and other procedures that my daughter faced. If I was calm and assured, her experience was very similar.

How Transformations Differ from Affirmations

Transformation literally means going beyond your form.

Wayne Dyer

The Empowerment Process is designed to work at a very deep level to bring about permanent life-changing results. Once you identify, acknowledge, and accept your issue or concern, you can make a quantum energy shift into self-empowerment.

An affirmation is a statement that puts your attention in a positive direction. The intention is a hopeful desire for the future. The Empowerment Process actually takes that "hope" and empowers you to actualize it to create a new, present, reality.

ATTRACTING WHAT YOU RESONATE WITH

If you resonate with something, that is what you attract, that is what your power will automatically draw to you. The goal is to attract what is for your highest benefit. Resonating with a disempowering belief such as, "I don't deserve to be successful," needs to be transformed so that you will draw what you do need to fulfill your goals. The Empowerment Process helps you make this transformation.

One of my clients wanted to advertise his skills in the local newspaper to bring in new business. However, for no clear reason he kept delaying. During his Empowerment Process session, he recognized his fear about being exposed to public scrutiny. He had grown up in a very critical family and was not ready to risk the possibility of others in a similar field judging him. He also feared they would see him as a competitor, as someone "stepping on their toes."

By transforming his disempowering energy he was able to bolster his self-esteem and resolve to go forward. When he felt ready, any reservations about advertising his services completely disappeared. His empowering statement actually went beyond "I deserve to be successful," to "I am success." It is not just about the words, but about what the physiology is able to energetically hold and manifest in action.

FULFILLING YOUR INTENTION THROUGH TRANSFORMATION

The Empowerment Process is not a left-brain mental activity addressing psychological issues. Rather, the process creates a holistic flow of energy for a high level of emotional integration. The transformation is clearly recognized and felt in the physiology. As your underlying issues surface during an Empowerment Process session, you transform and heal them to create a comfortable flow of energy resulting in a feeling of peace.

Empower yourself to create
a new present reality rather than a desired
hope for the future.

Addressing Physical Health Challenges

I am the physical system that steps down Divine light and "heavenizes" all of creation including myself.

Caroline Myss

Everyone desires maximum health and vitality. A balanced lifestyle and nutritious diet will support clarity of mind and physical energy. By getting the rest you need, and even having a spiritual practice, you will generally keep on top of life's challenges.

However, despite your vigilance, you may at times face health challenges, some debilitating or even life-threatening. Health issues might also be genetic, or the result of living in a toxic environment. Whatever the cause, strength and courage are required to confront and transform them.

LISTENING AND ATTENDING TO YOUR BODY'S MESSAGES

It is important to listen to your body's messages. Take the time to recognize a symptom before it becomes chronic or unbearable. Sometimes it is necessary to "put life on hold" to do the things necessary to regain your health. Patience and a positive attitude will help carry you through these trying times

I've helped facilitate physical healing through a variety of Empowerment Process transformations. Some changes were immediate; others took longer. It depends on the severity of the problem, karmic issues, and the readiness of the client to heal. All situations offer opportunities to learn. Welcoming your healing lessons with an open heart can support positive transformations.

One client, when planning a mountain trekking excursion, started growing painful plantar warts. A single Empowerment Process session, accompanied by other healing modalities brought about a transformation. The warts dried up and fell off in a matter of days. A similar event happened when my mom was scheduled for minor surgery to remove a chronically infected, calcified salivary gland. After a remote proxy session, she was able to dissolve it overnight. An x-ray, taken just before the scheduled surgery, revealed that the problem had magically disappeared. I have conducted several sessions where dangerously high blood pressure conditions normalized for clients.

TRUSTING WAYS TO SUPPORT YOUR HEALTH NEEDS

I wish I could say that all tumors and diseases could transform like this, but unfortunately that is not the case. My daughter's football-sized kidney tumor had to be shrunk with chemotherapy and removed surgically. But at least the energy work made her more comfortable. Some years ago, when in bed with gastritis for 13 weeks, I developed a great deal of patience and tolerance for pain, and rested more than I ever imagined I'd need. But I did heal thoroughly, and learned to stay in the present during a slow and gradual recovery. I supported the healing with the Empowerment Process, and was guided to relieve the pain. Shortly after healing I was off to a scheduled trip to China with no further incident or complication.

The reason for and source of physical injuries and diseases are not necessarily ever understood, but a positive attitude and balanced emotional response will support the healing process. I often assist others who seem to lose their equanimity and trust during those situations.

In her book, *Dying to Be Me,* Anita Moorjani relates that her healing miracle came as a near death experience which brought her back from "terminal" cancer to a complete, disease-free recovery. She experienced a total transformation for her to continue life on Earth. She now opens peoples' minds and hearts to greater possibilities of self-healing and self-love by sharing her experience and awareness.

The mind, body and spirit are intimately connected. When you transform on one level, the other levels also heal and shift. Whatever your physical challenge, the Empowerment Process is available to help you recognize your true power for self-healing.

© Photo by Deborah Roberts

Finding Support
to Get Through your Crisis

*When faced with a radical crisis, when the old way of being in
the world doesn't work anymore .... when survival is threat-
ened by seemingly insurmountable problems ... an individual
life-form will either die or rise above the limitations of its
condition through an evolutionary leap.*

Eckart Tolle

When you feel overwhelmed and unprepared to deal with life's
circumstances, you will benefit most from courageously and effectively addressing your concerns. The Empowerment Process
can help you in times of crisis. As long as you are willing to accept your situation, you can transform your discomfort. You will
be able to balance your emotions and stabilize your mind set to
support your physical well-being and strengthen your spirit.

The common, immediate reaction to a crisis is to emotionally
check-out, disappear and avoid facing the reality. Your fear challenges your equanimity, and anger generally follows. However,
avoidance just prolongs the agony. The Empowerment Process
helps you accept your feelings without resistance and successfully live through your crisis. Your reaction to the event will then
soften and you can gradually move out of your discomfort.

RECEIVING SUPPORT

It is important to ask for and receive the support you need. A crisis often involves some kind of a loss, one that affects your heart very deeply. Maybe your health is being challenged and you feel a loss of stamina, mobility or another faculty. Or, you've experienced the loss of a loved one through divorce or death and need to face shock, abandonment and grief. Maybe you have lost your job or some other financial support and feel destitute and fearful about your future. The resulting anxiety and worry, which can aggravate the symptoms you are experiencing, need to be addressed and transformed.

TRANSFORMING CORE BELIEFS

One of my clients came to me in a panic when she was diagnosed with a lump in her breast. She felt terrified to keep her medical appointment in case she might find out that she had breast cancer. Having a family history of this disease didn't help her fear level. The Empowerment Process gave her a chance to settle down and transform her core beliefs around being a victim. She had the lump removed with no sign of cancer and the event gave her the opportunity to dispel deep seated issues that she had carried for over 50 years. Her fear-based relationship with her sister, who had dealt with a mastectomy, was considerably healed. My client became mentally and emotionally healthier as a result of the scare. She feels gratitude for her life and lives more fully in the present.

The Empowerment Process can relieve the strong emotional impact from a life-crisis. Once you address and transform the stress and grief from a loss, you gain new perspective and energetic presence for greater stability and confidence. You come to realize that the traumatic event has created a new opportunity for growth in awareness, compassion, and understanding that serves all of life.

A life crisis creates a new opportunity
for growth in awareness, compassion
and understanding that serves all of life.

Staying Centered in Relationships

The purpose of a relationship is not to have another who might complete you, but to have another with whom you might share your completeness.

Neale Donald Walsch

The Empowerment Process is transformational work that helps you feel connected to yourself and integrated in mind, body, and spirit. Being centered requires inner stability. You want to maintain an unwavering openness to receive what you need without being swayed by external circumstances. When emotionally stable, you can trust your own feelings and respond to others from a secure sense of self.

OPENING TO SELF-LOVE

You will notice that when you transform emotionally charged issues and come into a state of balance, your physiology relaxes and your mind becomes clearer. Instead of always being in a reactive mode arising from your own unmet needs, you can listen, and respond appropriately to others. You'll find yourself more sensitive and loving.

One of my clients felt emotionally mistreated by his fiancé. Through Empowerment Process sessions, he was able to transform his energy and prevent continual confrontations and frustration in his relationship. During a session, he mentioned that his first three months of life were spent in an incubator and he wasn't nurtured as a premature newborn. This was the feeling that continued to play out as an insatiable neediness in his life.

The tremendous anger and frustration he was holding inside from not feeling nurtured influenced all of his relationships. The result was a lack of self-acceptance and a need for control. The Empowerment Process sessions opened him to higher understanding in general and a deeper appreciation of himself. He was able to stay centered and not misinterpret the behavior of his loved one. He developed the ability to love unconditionally without the expectations and demands of her having to fulfill his needs. That was something he could begin to do successfully for himself. The result was a sense of security and peace and a new perspective for living a fuller, more empowered life.

RESONATING WITH LIFE'S LESSONS

In all your relationships, you'll want to maximize your ability to give and receive love. That becomes much easier when you feel centered and peaceful inside. No matter what someone else's emotional needs or imbalances are, you can respond from your centered state. That way, you take nothing in as a personal affront. You recognize that they are only expressing their needs, even if not in a pleasant way.

Donald Epstein, developer of Network Chiropractic, writes in his book, The 12 Stages of Healing, "By moving through the 12 stages of healing, we gradually learn that we no longer take life, events, situations and other people so personally. Life provides us with lessons which can be difficult until we no longer resist them, but resonate with them."

Whenever your perspective on life depletes you, you feel unable to move forward, and even react negatively to things, the Empowerment Process can help you understand your resistances and transform them. You will then be able to feel a greater connection to yourself, others, and the great universal force behind it all.

Gaining Confidence to Follow your Intuition

Every test successfully met is rewarded by some growth in intuitive knowledge, strengthening of character, or initiation into a higher consciousness.

Paul Brunton

One goal of the Empowerment Process is to open your heart and mind to confidently flow with whatever life brings. Your intuitive sense is a natural ability that you use all the time without thinking about it. Learning to trust and use it more often can improve your ability to make clear, life-supportive decisions.

TRUSTING YOUR INFORMATION

Sometimes it feels like your intuition is urging you to take a risk - move to a new city, start a new job, get married, separate from a partner, follow your doctor's advice.

Life in freedom means having the courage to take the leap, and recognize when to be patient.

Through the Empowerment Process, you can move beyond

habitual limiting beliefs and allow your subtle sensory information to surface. That information, coming from your fine feeling level, is your intuitive sense. It isn't something you learn, it's something you trust. Even if it seems illogical, if it feels right, it usually is. If you have some lurking, undefined feeling not to go forward, listen to it. Timing is important. Change is constant, so pay attention to new information, unexpected events and internal cues.

RECOGNIZING YOUR INTUITIVE MESSAGES

Being open to your inner messaging means you are listening, listening to yourself – your heart, your mind, your body. Your heart is like a "truth meter," telling you how you feel about something. Your body, too, responds to messages, and will indicate where you need to put your attention. You just have to trust whatever information you receive.

One of my clients was ready to put a down payment on a condominium. She had come into an inheritance, and felt it was time to own a home. However, she felt some intuitive hesitation about the purchase, and came for a session. She realized that her wish to be outdoors in a quiet area was important; she needed garden space to raise plants and fulfill her passion to create healing oils. The willingness to be patient a little longer was the result of the transformation.

Within a week she was presented with an option to buy a house on a property that would fulfill all her desires. Her intuition had kept her from making a decision based on "thinking" something was a good idea. The Empowerment Process not only gave her the confidence to wait, but also clarified her commitment to her needs and trust in intuitive guidance.

FOLLOWING YOUR INTUITIVE GUIDANCE

You won't always "know" where life will take you, but The Empowerment Process can help you feel a heightened confidence and resolve to follow your intuitive guidance for energetic transformation. Living your life's passion becomes a joy.

In Penney Peirce's book, *The Intuitive Way,* she opens by saying "Living by intuition is an art that when mastered produces a thrill like no other. It brings us fluidity and joy, instantaneous answers, and abundant knowledge just for the asking."

When you follow your intuition, you tap the enormous potential of the non-linear, creative side of your brain, which is not bound by time and space. As Albert Einstein once said, "The intuitive mind is a sacred gift and the rational mind is a faithful servant." The universe can provide everything you need if you are listening. You will receive what you need and open to your own gifts for healing. So, put up your human antennae and listen in.

Connecting to Your Spiritual Path

What lies behind us, and what lies before us are tiny matters compared to what lies within us.

Ralph Waldo Emerson

Although the Empowerment Process is not a spiritual technique, it is designed to activate and facilitate your transformation so that you can explore and develop your gifts, achieve greater insights, and feel more connected to the great expanse of inner life. The spiritual level of your life is that unseen, magnificent soul which underlies all of life's experiences.

Through the Empowerment process you can experience a deep level of your more expanded self that is beyond any issue or suffering. You can stop defining yourself by who you know, what you own, what you do, and even what you think.

RECOGNIZING YOUR POWER IS WITHIN YOU

Once you feel that your life is no longer dependent on what happens on the outside, you can become more self-reliant and confident that your power comes from within you.

As Shakti Gawain says in her book, *The Path of Transformation,* to live a spiritual life is "to commit to living the integration of your human and spiritual aspects and learn to live as a whole being in balance and fulfillment on earth." Life always gives you opportunities to open to greater possibilities as you meet your challenges. The Empowerment Process can relieve you of burdens and open you to your own universal energy. That connection to your inner, spiritual nature is your greatest support system. Trust it to fulfill your desires and heal. You will recognize the shift in your energy as a sense of relief and contentment.

LOSING ATTACHMENT FOR OUTER CIRCUMSTANCES

Recently, a client set up his new website and began to attract lots of new business. He suddenly panicked when he felt unready to meet the challenge it presented to him. He was in a healing field himself, and yet he felt overwhelmed at the possibility of helping others. Through the Empowerment Process, he was able to transform his belief that he could never succeed and make money following his true passion. Once the old energy which held him back dropped off, he was inspired to fulfill his long awaited dream.

His experience in life had already prepared him to succeed. He just needed the confidence and self-esteem that energized him to go forward. During the session, he was able to appreciate himself at such a deep and expanded level that he didn't even feel attached to success. In his words, his ego seemed to disappear. Instead, he felt connected to his spiritual essence, his total universal self without expectation or concern about the results. Then he was ready to receive his clients from a safe, neutral space that had "nothing" to do with him.

SHARING YOUR GIFTS

Living in the present, like this, is where your greatest energy lies. From here, you can open to divine inspiration and share your gifts. You can not only experience your own healing, but express your energy to further a collective unity of purpose and planetary healing. The Empowerment Process can help you experience and enjoy your greatest potential that continues to unfold your divine purpose here on Earth.

Committing to the Journey

*When we commit ourselves to serving the process of life,
knowing that a treasure lies in every circumstance, then life
will mysteriously, miraculously bring us gifts.*

Donald Epstein

You have the special distinction of living your unique journey
on the planet at this time. You have come to fulfill a higher purpose, even make a difference in this world… to learn, to grow,
to share your gifts. As you pursue and allow for your inner healing, you will open to more and more creativity and inspiration.

BY SERVING YOURSELF YOU SERVE OTHERS

It really is your responsibility and maybe even your joy to accept
and respond to your challenges, not as bad luck or punishment
from God, but as thankful opportunities for your own personal
and spiritual growth. By serving yourself, you serve others. The
vibration of your energy and consciousness extends throughout the Earth and the Universe.

Probably, your greatest gift is in having a human body. It allows
you to function as an integrated whole, progress toward your

loftiest desires and fulfill your greatest potential. By recognizing and connecting to your innermost essence, you can move more easily with the flow of life.

In The 12 Stages of Healing, Donald Epstein lays out a systematic approach to understanding the path to wholeness. The 12th step is one in which you have done your healing work, let go of attachments and illusions, and come to rest in the spiritual recognition of who you really are. You are now ready to live an inspired life, enjoying and sharing new insights.

CONTINUING TO EXPRESS A GREATER POTENTIAL

There is no assurance of the future, or what you might meet around the next corner. But you can always take the opportunity to address what you might need to transform for further growth, happiness, and a deeper connection to yourself and others.

Transformation takes place not only according to what you desire, but what Nature, God and the Universe wants for all of us. As you continue to develop though your transformational experiences, you will come to function in a different way that serves everyone and everything. The Empowerment Process is a way to expand your energy every time you feel greater potential is available.

Commit to the journey knowing that support is there when you need it. Everyday can be a new beginning. I wish you a universe of love and light for your continued growth and empowerment.

Transformation takes place
not only according to what you desire,
but what Nature, God and the Universe
want for you.

Your Opportunities with the Empowerment Process

The Empowerment Process is available when you want to address and transform issues and concerns that seem to be holding you back in life. That includes anything that has been bothering you: long-standing emotional issues, health problems, career concerns, and desire for success in general. As you transform you'll find greater inner peace and growing appreciation of yourself and others.

WORKING WITH YOU

During individual sessions, I will work with you directly, in-person or on the phone, to help facilitate the energetic transformation necessary to address your concerns and pave the way for your next step of growth.

AN EMPOWERMENT PROCESS SESSION

If you are dealing with a specific issue and would like to make a significant, permanent transformation for healing, I will take you through the Empowerment Process. You will have the opportunity to address what is preventing you from moving forward so that you can release uncomfortable feelings including anxiety and fear. Whatever beliefs you hold that are not serving you can be shifted in order to establish a supportive foundation to meet your challenge. The result will be a clearer vision and new, positive energy to fulfill your purpose. As you are willing to resolve your issues and concerns, heal your emotional wounds, and open to your own spiritual growth, your inner conflicts will be resolved.

INTUITIVE GUIDANCE CONSULTATION

If you are unclear about your direction in life or find yourself at a critical decision point, I offer intuitive guidance consultations to identify what you need to resolve in order to go the next step. During the session I will connect with your higher self to uncover the qualities and influences in your life that are having an impact on your current situation. The result will be like a road map to give you the direction you need to make choices. In some cases, a multi-dimensional template will unfold so you can recognize who you are at a deeper level and make sense out of a current feeling or situation. Information may present itself regarding the perfect timing to make a decision. Sometimes an Empowerment Process session will naturally follow once you are clear that you have something ready to transform and heal.

TO SCHEDULE AN APPOINTMENT

For an individual session, go to http://EmpowermentProcess. com/individual-sessions/

EMPOWERMENT PROCESS WORKSHOPS

You can learn to facilitate the Empowerment Process in a week-end workshop. Currently there are two courses available - the fundamental course, *Following Your Intuitive Guidance for Energetic Transformation,* and a follow-up course, *Balancing Your Chakras for Energetic Transformation.* Each one comes with a book of materials to support your learning and continued practice. Although you will learn principles of transformation, the basic workshop is primarily experiential so that you gain the skill and confidence to facilitate the process for yourself as well as for others. There will be many additional opportunities for practice and learning which I will be presenting via the internet. You will be able to receive continuing podcasts and live webinars including on-line facilitations. Check my website for course dates and locations and follow my YouTube channel for continued inspiration and education.

MENTORING PROGRAMS

If you feel your life situation needs on-going attention and support, I offer Empowerment Process packages which give you the opportunity to receive continuous transformation through individual Empowerment Process sessions and Intuitive Guidance Consultations. Each mentoring package is tailor-made so that individuals have the integration time and appropriate number of sessions to achieve resolution.

TESTIMONIALS

There are hundreds of testimonials from individual clients and from workshop participants. Many are posted on my website and continue to come in regularly through e-mails, texts, and voice messages. There is always an excitement and feeling of inspiration when you overcome your challenges and meet your goals. I welcome the sharing of that empowerment.

My personal goal is to inspire others to become self-sufficient. Everyone has the inherent ability to heal and empower themselves. It just takes the willingness to open to positive change.

You can view testimonials on my website:
www.EmpowermentProcess.com.

The universe presents new paths

for discovery

every day.

About Janet

Janet is the developer and teacher of the Empowerment Process. She has provided sessions to thousands of people worldwide from all walks of life who are open to personal transformation and growth. In addition, hundreds of people who have taken her fundamental course, *Following Your Intuitive Guidance for Energetic Transformation,* continue to enjoy the ability to create personal transformations for themselves as well as facilitate sessions for their friends and their own clients.

Janet's individual Empowerment Process sessions and Intuitive Reading consultations are generally offered long-distance by phone. She also teaches the Empowerment Process courses, *Following Your Intuitive Guidance* and *Balancing Your Chakras.*

Janet offers Empowerment Process sessions to those open to personal transformation and growth, letting go of "stories" and disempowering beliefs that keep them from fulfilling their passions and missions in life. Her mentoring program and facilitator training courses are available for people to deepen their experience and understanding of personal transformation.

You can follow her on Facebook, Linked-in, Twitter, and on her YouTube Channel which continue to broadcast her message and present educational material for your empowerment.

A copy of this book in paperback is available through Amazon Books.

For individual sessions, course schedules, to order the book, or find her on social media, go to www.EmpowermentProcess.com.

Janet Swartz, creator of the Empowerment Process® and Empowerment Process courses.

Janet has a rare gift of being able to support people in times of crisis and change. She can help those who are open to transformation and growth remove their doubts and fears. With their energy shift comes a new integration of balanced emotions, physical well-being and spiritual connection.

Her love and compassion, combined with her own passion to serve, gives people the comfort and confidence to heal, fulfill their desires and discover their life's purpose.

"The smile on my face began to hurt because it lasted so long. As we mature, we sometimes lose faith in people, so I was somewhat skeptical going into our session. Janet gave me the opportunity to rethink and reposition heavy, negative thoughts I'd been carrying with me for a very long time. Those same negative thoughts no longer have the strong hold on me that they once did, and I'm able to have deeper, more meaningful conversations with the people I love. Janet surprised me because she opened my eyes and expanded my awareness in ways I'd not previously considered. She helped me to move myself out of the way of progress." —JN-California

The Empowerment Process® — Discover a Way to Transform and Heal is a powerful discourse on what it means to transform and take responsibility for one's own healing and happiness. The process is available through her individual sessions and can be learned in her fundamental course, **Following Your Intuitive Guidance for Energetic Transformation.**

There is no place like home, and that is within you. Explore the rooms and enjoy the beauty.

ISBN-13: 978-1499352689

Made in USA - Crawfordsville, IN
10018_9781499352689
10.21.2020 1600